EVERYDAY HEROES

By

LAURIE BROOKS

Dramatic Publishing

Woodstock, Illinois • England • Australia • New Zealand

For Joanna, Liz and Stephanie, three everyday heroes.

IMPORTANT BILLING AND CREDIT REQUIREMENTS

* * * *

Everyday Heroes received its equity premiere at The Coterie Theatre, Kansas City, Mo., March 2, 2004.

CAST

Win	Sam Cordes
Jo Judson	Andi Meyer
Shawna	Angela Wildflower Polk
Kurt	Richard Stubblefield
Cash McKenzie/Ms. Branch/Dr. Krakauer	Heidi VanMiddlesworth
Payton Powers/Raphael Jimenez	Sam Wright

PRODUCTION STAFF AND CREW

Director	Jeff Church
Set Design	Jason Harris
Costume Design	Georgiana Londre
Lighting Design	Art Kent
Sound Design	David Kiehl
Stage Manager	Amy Abels Owen

The Olympic Arts Festival, Kennedy Center Imagination Celebration of Salt Lake City, in partnership with the University of Utah's Department of Theatre, presented the world premiere of *Everyday Heroes*.

CAST

Win	Chris Johnston
Kurt	Tyler Johnson
Shawna	Sheryl Nichols
Jo Judson	Shana Wiersum
Payton Powers/Raphael Jimenez	Eric McGraw
Cash McKenzie/Ms. Branch/Dr. Krakauer	Shannon Hollinger

PRODUCTION STAFF AND CREW

Director	Margo Andrews
Producer	David Dynak
Assistant Director/Stage Manager	Linda L. Brown
Set Design/Technical Director	S. Glen Brown
Lighting Design	Megan McCormick
Costume Design	Brenda Van der Wiel
Sound Design	Brian Burchett
Fight Choreography	Paul Kiernan
Camera Operators	Mario Mendez, Justin Morris, Bethany Johnson

* * * *

Special thanks to Jeff Church, David Dynak, Margo Andrews, Janet Wolf, Elaine S. Harding, retired firefighter Glen Judson, Lieutenant Dave Schulman, Nassau County Police Department, Diane Lutz, and Elise and Jerry Lazar.

FROM THE PLAYWRIGHT:

The most compelling theatre raises questions rather than determines answers. Good theatre begins a dialogue that lingers long after the lights have dimmed on the action in the theatre space. If the questions are compelling enough, the debates that grow out of them can have a lasting effect, changing viewpoints and altering attitudes. No one knew this better than the Greeks, who developed a theatre that would instruct its people on how to conduct their lives through demonstrating the consequences of ill-chosen actions.

This play grew out of my desire to pursue three questions: What happens in the aftermath of heroism, if the hero harbors a terrible secret? How does the frequently distorted truth of the media become more valid than reality? What are the consequences of society's silencing of the emotional lives of young men? From these ideas, the character Win Lawrence emerged, a young man who finds himself lauded as a hero but knows his heroism is predicated on lies. Even as he becomes a media darling, he is torn between two equal forces—loyalty to his family and the insistent voice of his own conscience.

As Win explores his choices and makes his decisions, I hope his journey will raise questions for you—questions about the creation of truth and lies, loyalty and survival, obligations to others and to ourselves—and begin a dialogue between friends, parents and children, teachers and students that will extend the life of the play long after the last words of the performance. Ironically, this play was created during the summer prior to 9/11. The events of that terrible day redefined our perceptions of heroism, and made us aware that everyday heroes are always among us.

EVERYDAY HEROES

A Full-length Play

CHARACTERS:

WIN . . . . 16 years old
KURT. . . . . 18 years old, Win's brother
SHAWNA . . . . 16 years old, Win's friend
JO JUDSON. 30, female firefighter
ACTOR I (female) . . . . . Cash McKenzie, Ms. Branch, Dr. Krakauer
ACTOR II (male) . . . . . . Payton Powers, Raphael Jimenez
CAMERA OPERATOR I (male or female)
CAMERA OPERATOR II (optional) (male or female)

TIME: The present.

• The play takes place on a bare stage. At center is a raised platform with steps that rise to a smaller platform with a door. Somewhere on the platform is a television set.

• A live camera (and camera person) projects the news scenes as they occur, creating a simultaneous broadcast of the action. Thus, the audience sees the action in two ways: as the actors play it and simultaneous close-up projections. These projections are sometimes skewed, distorted, not quite real. There is a sense that the news and the newspeople are larger than life.

• The lyrics to the Nightshade theme are included in the play. Producers may create their own music.

• Two large U.S. maps are hung on stage with red marked routes that crisscross the country. On the platform throughout the play is a packed duffle bag.

• TV news characters remain on stage throughout the play, watching the action. No effort is made to conceal their doubling as other characters. These additional characters are created through actors' posture and voice.

EVERYDAY HEROES

(WIN in spotlight.)

WIN. Most of the time I try to be invisible. I go to school, study, do my chores, take care of my mother. I do what's expected of me and keep my head down. Try not to call too much attention to myself. That's in the day-time. At night, I dream. And even though the dreams are different, they're always the same. I'm traveling. On the road to somewhere and no one cares. No, that's good, because then I don't have to feel bad because I'm leaving. Most of the time I'm on this monster black Harley, the engine humming underneath me, screaming down the highway. All the small towns look the same—banks, hardware stores, supermarkets. But here's the best part, nobody knows who I am. I could be anybody. Anybody at all. Invisible.

(LIGHTS cross-fade. WIN studies a map. Enter KURT.)

KURT. Guess what, Boy Scout.
WIN. You won the lottery.
KURT. Almost as good. I'm starting in the game tomor-row. *(Sports announcer voice.)* Here's Kurt Lawrence on the mound. He winds up...and there's the pitch. Stee-rike! Looks like a no-hitter today, Bob. Tell us, Mr.

Lawrence, how does it feel to be the hottest young pitcher in baseball? Well, Bob, baseball's been very, very good to me.

WIN. Oh, you're good. Real intelligent.

KURT. That's right. I am good. Today is the beginning of a star in the making.

WIN. I washed your uniform.

KURT. Good. What's today's route?

WIN. The Appalachian Trail, all the way from North Carolina to Upstate New York. People hike it.

KURT. Why would anyone want to walk that far when you can drive?

WIN. Never mind.

KURT. Gold mining in California, climbing the red rocks or whatever in Arizona… I don't get it.

WIN. It's called adventure, Kurt. Here. You gotta sign these papers for me.

KURT. What are they?

WIN. Stupid forms that say I'll follow the rules of the classroom. *(KURT signs.)*

KURT. Like you wouldn't. Hey, I'm getting pretty good at this forging. Looks just like her signature. All those loopy letters and everything.

WIN. The telephone company called again.

KURT. You tell 'em she wasn't home?

WIN. Yeah, but they didn't buy it. So I told 'em she sent the check yesterday.

KURT. Good. Where is she?

WIN. Upstairs.

KURT. Did you check on her when you got home?

WIN. Yeah, I checked on her.

KURT. Well?

WIN. She was sleeping.

KURT. At three o'clock?

WIN. She was up earlier. It's just a nap.

KURT. She was okay at lunch?

WIN. Yeah. I made her some soup.

KURT. Did she eat?

WIN. Yeah. She's doing good.

KURT. Okay. Okay. Did you remember to check her room again?

WIN. Every inch. Nothing. It's clean.

KURT. You check the bathroom?

WIN. I ought to know the drill by now. Besides, she's gonna make it this time. I know it.

KURT. Yeah, I've heard that one before.

WIN. She went to that counselor, didn't she? And she ironed.

KURT. She what?

WIN. She ironed my shirt.

KURT. She ironed your shirt.

WIN. I'll ask her to do one of yours tomorrow.

KURT. I can iron my own shirts.

WIN. I think this time is different, Kurt. She wants to stop. For us.

KURT. For you, Boy Scout.

WIN. What are you talking about?

KURT. Do you think she'd do it for me? *(Silence.)* Like she'd ever iron my shirts.

WIN. I believe her this time.

KURT. Don't. Don't be stupid.

WIN. It's not stupid.

KURT. How many times has she promised you?

WIN. Why can't you be hopeful for once? It wouldn't kill you.

KURT. Hopeful? That's a candy-ass word if I ever heard one. Because I'm not "hopeful." Why do you talk like that?

WIN. Sorry. I forgot how confusing two-syllable words are for you.

KURT. Shut up, Boy Scout.

WIN. Here. You gotta sign this one, too. *(KURT signs.)* Aren't you gonna ask me what you're signing?

KURT. No. I'm not. I trust you.

WIN. I went to the store and got those cookies you like.

KURT. Good. I could eat a couple thousand. That girl called again last night. Sharon or something.

WIN. Shawna?

KURT. That's it.

WIN. What'd she say?

KURT. She wanted to talk to you, that's all.

WIN. Did she say she'd call back?

KURT. No.

WIN. Did she leave her number?

KURT. No.

WIN. Thanks for asking.

KURT. I didn't know it was important. Where's the car keys?

WIN. In the freezer.

KURT. That's a new one.

WIN. She found 'em in the lamp. She got halfway down the driveway before I stopped her.

KURT. I better keep 'em on me for now.

WIN. Kurt?

KURT. Yeah.

WIN. Mom wants to come to your game.

KURT. I don't want her at the game.

WIN. I'll watch her. I'll make sure she's okay.

KURT. Not good enough.

WIN. I won't even let her have a jump-starter. Not even if she begs.

KURT. No. Not one more time.

WIN. Give her a chance, Kurt.

KURT. A chance? Like the chance when she got so trashed that I had to walk her home because she was too falling-down drunk to drive? How about the chance when she laughed so loud that no one could hear the game? How about so drunk she propositioned the coach for a little fun after the game?

WIN. That's a lie. You didn't hear what she said to him.

KURT. No, but a few hundred other people did. Why do you always stick up for her? You don't owe her anything. She's just the woman who gave birth to us. And that was our bad luck.

WIN. Shut up, Kurt.

KURT. A couple sober days and you think you're in Disney World. Come on, Mom, let's ride the merry-go-round.

WIN. Shut up, Kurt, I mean it.

KURT. Get back. He's getting mad. Is the Boy Scout pissed off? Guess he's not "hopeful" anymore. *(WIN charges his brother. They fall to the floor. KURT quickly overpowers WIN.)* What do you have to say now, Boy Scout?

WIN. Get off me.

KURT. Not until you say you won't trust her. I didn't spend all this time and energy raising you up so that you could blow it for both of us. We've managed to get this far without a major disaster and I aim to keep it that way.

WIN. Get off me. *(WIN struggles.)*

KURT. Okay, Boy Scout. Get up. *(KURT releases WIN.)* You're gonna have to get a lot tougher or you're gonna get eaten alive. If she doesn't kill you those thugs at school will. If you're smart you'll listen to me and take my advice.

WIN. I know. I know.

KURT. Get yourself a posse, some friends.

WIN. I got friends.

KURT. Yeah, a coupla girls and that geek, what's his name.

WIN. I don't choose my friends by how many fights they win.

KURT. Easy for you to say. I got your back. That's my job. But I won't be around forever.

WIN. I know.

KURT. I just want to be sure you don't go into la-la land with Mom. She's not going to get better. I don't care what she promises.

WIN. You don't know that for sure.

KURT. Yes, I do. A couple more years and you can have that adventure. In the meantime, I got to get to bed early. You got mom detail tonight.

WIN. It's your turn.

KURT. I got the game tomorrow. I gotta get some sleep.

WIN. I was going out tonight.

KURT. So go out. Just don't be late. I'll watch her till you get home. Then you take over.

WIN. Okay, but you owe me.

KURT. I don't owe you squat. *(KURT picks WIN up and swings him around. SOUND of breaking glass. Everything stops.)* Now look what you did.

WIN. I did?

KURT. Never mind. Get outa here. I gotta get this cleaned up.

WIN. I'll help. We both did it.

KURT. Get out. *(SOUND of MOM's voice calling, "Win!")* She's coming. Get out!

WIN. No fighting, okay?

KURT. Okay. Hurry up. *(WIN moves to exit.)* Win.

WIN. Yeah?

KURT. Don't bring her to my game.

(LIGHTS cross-fade. Night. KURT watches TV. Simultaneous, overlapping PROJECTIONS of the news scenes are seen. TV news. MUSIC.)

CASH MCKENZIE. In today's world it's even more important to stay on top of what's happening, to keep informed on the events of the day as they unfold. When you want to know, we keep you in the know. I'm Cash McKenzie, and I'll tell it like it is, no holds barred.

PAYTON POWERS. And I'm Payton Powers. I'll take you to the heart of the story, throw open the windows of truth and give you the bottom line. All the news, guests, innovations, trends and events, weather and traffic. Every day. All day.

CASH MCKENZIE. On the Everyday Show…what you need to know…

PAYTON POWERS. …the way you want it told.

VOICE-OVER. Payton Powers and Cash McKenzie, your friends in the news.
KURT. My friends in the news.

(Outside SOUNDS of laughter, joking. KURT clicks off TV. PROJECTIONS out. Enter WIN.)

WIN. What are you doing up?
KURT. Mom detail.
WIN. It's not late.
KURT. Never mind.
WIN. Is she all right?
KURT. *She's* all right.
WIN. What happened to your face?
KURT. I told you not to be "hopeful." It's the same thing all over again. Just another happy day at home.
WIN. What happened?
KURT. I was trying to sleep but this crashing woke me up, so I came upstairs. And what do you think I saw? She was sitting at the kitchen table, downing shots. I was right about her, Boy Scout, I knew she'd never quit. A thousand promises that add up to zero. Right then, looking at her, I saw my future stretching out like some endless highway. You and me tied to her for the rest of our lives.
WIN. Shit! Did you fight?
KURT. What do you think? I poured the rest of the bottle down the sink. She came at me. I put my arms up to block her punches, but she got one past me and connected…right here. When I got up I…I just lost it. I shook her and shook her and shook her. She looked right

at me. God, she looked like a wild animal. Then she just went limp. Passed out, I guess.

WIN. Is she all right?

KURT. Yeah, she's all right.

WIN. I'll go check on her.

KURT. She's sleeping. I carried her upstairs and put her to bed. She's out cold. *(Car horn honks.)*

WIN. They're waiting for me.

KURT. You're not going anywhere. I've gotta get some sleep.

WIN. I won't be long, Kurt.

KURT. I'm done with mom detail tonight.

WIN. You said yourself she's out cold. We're gonna pick up Shawna. She's waiting for me.

KURT. Boy Scout likes a girl.

WIN. Give me a break, Kurt.

KURT. No, you give me a break. I got a game tomorrow. *(Car horn honks.)*

WIN. I gotta go.

KURT. Wait. There is a solution. *(KURT takes a key out of his pocket.)*

WIN. Put the key away. I'm not locking her in again.

KURT. Why not? It worked before. She's passed out anyway. She won't wake up until morning.

WIN. It's not right.

KURT. Right? Is it right that she breaks her promises? Is it right that she controls our lives? Don't talk to me about what's right. *(Car honks again.)* Shut up. He's coming. *(Pause.)* Look. You can unlock the door when you get home.

WIN. What if she wakes up and finds out?

KURT. I told you, she's out cold.

WIN. I don't know.

KURT. Then stay home with her for the rest of your life. I'm going to bed.

WIN. Wait. Wait.

KURT. What?

WIN. You really think it'll be okay?

KURT. I think when she wakes up she won't know what planet she's on. Just don't be out too late.

(WIN exits. LIGHTS cross-fade. SOUNDS of laughing young people, car doors slamming, driving away. IMAGES of fire. SOUNDS of fire—crackling, burning, hissing. Smoke. TV NEWS MUSIC. PROJECTIONS. SOUND of police band radio reporting the fire. Multiple, overlapping voices of news reporters.)

Late-breaking news report… This just in…a teenager…a fire…a daring rescue…we're here at the scene of the fire… Four-alarm blaze…119 Trevor Place… Fire erupted on the second floor just past midnight…in the Woodlawn Park section of the city…described as a smoke-filled inferno…

(Sirens. KURT and WIN are seen in the smoke. The two boys struggle. WIN pushes KURT. He falls. A firefighter (JO JUDSON) passes through the smoke. She tackles WIN to the ground. He gets up, pummels her. She prevents him from re-entering the fire. WIN screams once, "Mom!" LIGHTS cross-fade. TV NEWS MUSIC. PROJECTIONS.)

CASH MCKENZIE. And we're back with more on the Woodlawn Park fire. Payton Powers files this report from the scene. Payton?

PAYTON POWERS. The fire broke out sometime after midnight in this small house at 119 Trevor Place in the rundown Woodlawn Park section of the city. Firefighters responded quickly to bring the fire under control but the house is devastated. Marianne Lawrence, forty-one, who was inside the house at the time of the fire, was rushed to Mercy Hospital where she is listed in critical condition. Fires in this part of the city are not uncommon but the actions of young Winston Lawrence during the fire are anything but typical. With us at the scene is Sergeant Jo Judson.

JO. That's Lieutenant Judson.

PAYTON POWERS. Of course. Lieutenant Judson. I understand there was a daring rescue tonight. Can you tell us the details?

JO. There were three people in the house when the fire started—Marianne Lawrence and her two sons. The youngest kid, Winston, pulled his older brother, Kurt, out of the fire.

PAYTON POWERS. What is Kurt's condition, Lieutenant?

JO. He was taken to the hospital, but I think he'll be all right.

PAYTON POWERS. What were the circumstances of the rescue?

JO. We're not sure yet. When we arrived at the scene Winston had already pulled his brother out of the fire so our priority was rescuing Mrs. Lawrence who was still inside. We pulled her out of a second-story bedroom. That kid, Winston, would have gone back in for his mother if we hadn't stopped him. We had to hold him back while we pulled her out.

PAYTON POWERS. Marianne Lawrence was rushed to Mercy Hospital. Do you have an update on her condition, Lieutenant?

JO. Sorry, I don't.

PAYTON POWERS. Is there any information on what caused the fire?

JO. There'll be an investigation. But until then it's just speculation.

PAYTON POWERS. You've been twice decorated for bravery in the line of duty, Lieutenant.

JO. Just doing my job.

PAYTON POWERS. Would you consider Winston Lawrence's behavior typical? How do family members usually respond when confronted with an emergency like this?

JO. People usually panic or freeze.

PAYTON POWERS. Lieutenant Judson, would you call Winston Lawrence's actions heroic?

JO. Definitely. But civilians should stay out of the way and let us do our jobs. *(JO fades.)*

PAYTON POWERS. Thanks for joining us, Lieutenant Judson. There you have it, Cash. A teenager named a hero by a hero. This is Payton Powers in Woodlawn Park. Back to you, Cash.

CASH MCKENZIE. Thank you, Payton. Marianne Lawrence, forty-one, remains in Mercy Hospital, where she is listed in critical condition. Kurt Lawrence is being treated for a head wound and Winston Lawrence is being treated for minor burns. The cause of the fire is as yet unknown. We'll follow the story.

(PROJECTIONS out. LIGHTS cross-fade. Night. SOUND of WIN's MOTHER calling his name as if from far away. The emergency room. WIN sleeps, dreams, mumbles in his sleep, moans, cries out.)

KURT. Win! Wake up. Wake up.

WIN. Kurt?

KURT. Hey. Let go. You're okay. You were having another bad dream. We're at the hospital.

WIN. Mom?

KURT. No change.

WIN. Can we see her now?

KURT. They said we should wait. *(Silence.)*

WIN. Your head?

KURT. Killing me.

WIN. Mine, too.

KURT. It's a carbon monoxide headache from eating the smoke. The doctor told me.

WIN. I'm sorry I pushed you.

KURT. That's the last time I piss you off.

WIN. It's not funny.

KURT. I'm okay, Boy Scout. You got me out. *(Silence.)*

WIN. It's my fault. The whole thing was my fault.

KURT. Mom started the fire. Not you. She was probably smoking in bed again.

WIN. But where did she get the smokes? I checked her room before I went out. It was clean.

KURT. Who knows where she hid 'em.

WIN. But we locked her door, Kurt. She couldn't get out.

KURT. She probably never woke up.

WIN. What if she did and she was trying to get out?

KURT. Shut up. How could we know she'd set the place
    on fire?
HOSPITAL PA ANNOUNCEMENT. Dr. David Bull. Dr.
    David Bull, please call the operator.
KURT. Did you tell them anything?
WIN. Who?
KURT. I don't know. Anybody. The cops. The EMS guys.
    Think.
WIN. No. I didn't say anything.
KURT. Good. Keep your mouth shut.
WIN. Do you think they'll question us?
KURT. I don't know but if they do, don't tell them any-
    thing. It's none of their business. Just play the good boy.
    You know how to do that. They'll forget all about it in a
    few days. Like it never happened.
WIN. I wish it never happened.
KURT. Too late for that.
HOSPITAL PA ANNOUNCEMENT. Dr. Robert Nichols
    report to ICU. Dr. Nichols to ICU.
WIN. They're not going to forget about it, Kurt. They in-
    terviewed that firefighter on TV.
KURT. So?
WIN. So they're making a big deal of it. Won't they think
    it's weird if we won't talk to them?
KURT. Yeah. You're right. For a change. We gotta talk to
    'em.
WIN. We should tell the truth and get it over with.
KURT. Are you crazy? We locked her in. They might
    charge us.
WIN. Charge us with what?
KURT. I don't know. Attempted murder or something.
WIN. But we didn't set the fire.

KURT. You think they'll believe that? The whole town knows what she's like. *(Silence.)* We can't tell the truth. So forget it.

WIN. That firefighter called me heroic on TV.

KURT. So?

WIN. So, it's not true, that's all.

KURT. You got me out, didn't you?

HOSPITAL PA ANNOUNCEMENT. Code blue. Code blue. Dr. Evan Wichosky to ICU stat.

WIN. Why did you stop me? We could have got her out.

KURT. You might have killed yourself.

WIN. You could have helped me.

KURT. I'm not dying for her. And you aren't either. We did enough. Now we got to get through this.

WIN. Do you think she'll die?

KURT. I don't know.

(LIEUTENANT JUDSON appears, overhears the following.)

WIN. If she dies…

KURT. What?

WIN. I'll never forgive myself…or you, either.

(LIGHTS cross-fade. TV NEWS MUSIC. PROJECTIONS take on a level of distortion.)

PAYTON POWERS. And we're back with the Everyday Show, what you need to know, the way you want it told. I'm Payton Powers.

CASH MCKENZIE. …and I'm Cash McKenzie. Joining us today is Winston Lawrence, sixteen, who risked his life to save his older brother, Kurt, when their Woodlawn Park home caught fire last night, then faced danger a second time in an attempt to help his mother. Welcome, young man. I heard you like to be called Win.

WIN. Yeah. Win.

CASH MCKENZIE. Well, Win, first let me say that we are all hoping for your mother's speedy recovery, that she'll be home with you boys soon.

WIN. Thank you.

CASH MCKENZIE. Tell us in your own words what happened the night of the fire.

WIN. Well, I got home around midnight. The house was filled with smoke. I found my brother unconscious near the bottom of the stairs. I got him on my back and carried him out of the house. Once we were out in the yard and I knew he was all right, I tried to go back for my mom.

PAYTON POWERS. With me in the studio is Kurt Lawrence, who was rescued by his brother, Win, hero of the Woodlawn Park fire. Kurt, you were at home when the fire broke out. What happened that night?

KURT. Hey, Payton. I love your show.

PAYTON POWERS. Tell us what happened the night of the fire.

KURT. I went to bed early that night. I had a game the next day. I pitch for the Warriors. We're five and O. Go, Warriors! I woke up and realized something was wrong. I came upstairs, my bedroom's in the basement, and I felt the heat. I headed for my mom's room, to save her, you know. I was going up the stairs, I couldn't see my hand in front of my face the smoke was so thick, but then the ceiling collapsed, I guess, because something hit my head and the next thing I remember I woke up in the hospital.

PAYTON POWERS. That's when you heard that your brother, Win, had rescued you.

KURT. Yeah. That was cool.

PAYTON POWERS. Kurt, do you remember anything about the rescue?

KURT. No, nothing.

PAYTON POWERS. Do you remember seeing your brother on the stairs?

KURT. No, I don't. I don't remember anything.

PAYTON POWERS. Are you close to your brother?

KURT. Yeah, sure. We're a lot alike. I look out for him, you know.

PAYTON POWERS. I guess this time he looked out for you.

CASH MCKENZIE. When you tried to re-enter the house, Win, someone stopped you.

WIN. Yeah. Lieutenant Judson.

CASH MCKENZIE. Lieutenant Judson was impressed with your bravery, young man. *(Silence.)* Am I embarrassing you?

WIN. Yes, ma'am.

CASH MCKENZIE. There's nothing embarrassing about being a hero. Fire officials have determined that the fire started in your mother's bedroom, is that correct?

WIN. I think it was the wiring or something. It's an old house.

PAYTON POWERS. Kurt, I'd like to know more about your relationship with your brother. Do you ever fight?

KURT. No. We get along great. Like I said I look out for him.

PAYTON POWERS. Has your brother ever done anything heroic before?

KURT. I don't know about heroic. He's a good kid. Always helping Mom and me.

CASH MCKENZIE. They say you never know how you'll react in desperate circumstances. Given what you know now, if this happened again, what would you do differently?

WIN. I would have got my mom out.

PAYTON POWERS. Kurt, what have you said to your brother to thank him?

KURT. Thanks, bro, for being a hero.

CASH MCKENZIE. Win, did you ever think you'd become a hero?

WIN. No, ma'am. I'm not really a hero.

KURT. I would have done exactly the same thing my brother did. Anyone would.

PAYTON POWERS. Thank you, Kurt Lawrence. One young man who knows the true meaning of brotherly love.

CASH MCKENZIE. Thank you, Win Lawrence, a young man who claims he's not a hero, but who others say exemplifies the very best young people have to offer. Now we take a short commercial break. When we return, perfect abs in three weeks. We'll tell you how. Stay with us.

(LIGHTS cross-fade. PROJECTIONS out. A motel room. KURT lounges. WIN listens intently to a police band radio. SHAWNA enters.)

SHAWNA. Is Win Lawrence here?

KURT. There's someone here to see you, Boy Scout.

SHAWNA. The name's Shawna.

WIN. Shawna!

SHAWNA. That's me. So, are you gonna ask me in, or what?

WIN. Yeah, come in.

SHAWNA. Is this place safe? I hate cockroaches.

WIN. The insurance company's putting us up.

SHAWNA. My God, I had to see you. I had to tell you how amazing I think you are. The most amazing person I know. A real hero. Not made up or anything.

WIN. Don't believe everything you hear on the news. *(KURT moves to exit. SHAWNA turns down the radio.)* Hey. Where you going?

KURT. Out of here. *(KURT exits.)*

SHAWNA. What's with him?

WIN. I don't know.

SHAWNA. I saw you on TV. You looked so good. Hot. My God, you're famous. You risked your life to save someone. Just like Nightshade. But you, you're right here, right now, a real hero. Oh, I brought you the math homework. Let me tell you, you haven't missed a thing. It just keeps getting worse. Those kids are all like, I finished before you. No, you didn't, I did. I'm the smartest. No, I am. We're all the smartest because we're in Math Three Accelerated. What? I just want to strangle them all. They're so immature. I went to see my guidance counselor and told him, you've got to move me, I don't care where, even math for dummies, I can't stand those kids another day. When are you coming back to school?

WIN. Never, I hope.

SHAWNA. Let's run away. I hear California's nice, warm and sunny all the time. Of course, they have earth-quakes. I know, how about Hawaii? Waterfalls and flowers and stuff.

WIN. Too plastic. How about Sedona?

SHAWNA. What?

WIN. The red rock canyons of Arizona. In Sedona.

SHAWNA. Okay. I'll go.

WIN. When?

SHAWNA. Now.

WIN. My bag's already packed.

SHAWNA. They won't miss me. I cut all the time and never get in trouble. If you have a ninety-six average, they don't care what you do.

WIN. They haven't even called here.

SHAWNA. If you were a kid with bad grades they would have called. You can bet on that. Besides, life learning is more important and I have life learning to do here. I knew you were a real hero. I just knew it, ever since you got those losers off my back.

WIN. It's temporary, believe me.

SHAWNA. I never really got a chance to thank you. Too many people around. *(SHAWNA moves suggestively close to him.)*

WIN. Look, Shawna, you don't have to...

SHAWNA. I want to. You didn't have to stand up to them like that.

WIN. Yes, I did. I couldn't let them hassle you.

SHAWNA. Yeah. But they might have kicked your ass.

WIN. They're all bark and no bite.

SHAWNA. Maybe they'll fall into a gigantic hole and get sucked down into the epicenter of the earth. I saw that on Nightshade. Cretins. That's what they are. Want to walk down to the One Stop for coffee? Maybe we'll be photographed together by the paparazzi. *(WIN hesitates.)* Oh. That's okay. I don't blame you. Guess you wouldn't want anyone to draw conclusions about…you and me.

WIN. It's not that, Shawna.

SHAWNA. I understand. Now that you're famous and all.

WIN. That's not it.

SHAWNA. It's not?

WIN. No. I'd like to go for coffee. Just not right now.

SHAWNA. Oh, my God, I'm sorry. I'm such an insensitive idiot. You must be freaked after what you've been through.

WIN. I'm fine.

SHAWNA. You're so brave. If you weren't a hero, you'd be freaked. Okay, let's stay here and watch Nightshade. I've got a tape with me. I've seen all the episodes already but I still watch them.

WIN. I've got the radio on.

SHAWNA. That's boring. *(SHAWNA puts in the tape.)* You ever seen Nightshade?

WIN. Once. Not really.

SHAWNA. What! *(TV announcer's voice on TV.)* "Into this world of crime and criminals there is one who harnesses the power of good. Nightshade!" Look, Win. *(SHAWNA shows him she is wearing a Nightshade T-shirt.)* There she is. Strong and brave and beautiful. She's my hero. And you, now, of course. Hey, let's see if you're on the news again.

WIN. Shawna.

SHAWNA. What?

WIN. You're wacked. You know that?

SHAWNA. Sure I do. Who wants to be normal? Let's watch the all-news station. I can't believe you're on TV. A real celebrity.

WIN. Shawna. I need to hear the radio.

SHAWNA. What! There I go again. Just can't help myself. *(Pause.)* You must be tired. All those interviews and everything.

WIN. I can't sleep. I keep having these dreams.

SHAWNA. What kind of dreams? Maybe I could analyze them for you. I've got this book, *Revealing Yourself: The True Meaning of your Dreams*.

WIN. No, thanks.

SHAWNA. Did your ears get burned? God, look at your eyebrows. Well, what's left of them. Does it hurt?

WIN. Not too much.

SHAWNA. Hey. You want to run away with me? For real?

WIN. Yeah, sure.

SHAWNA. Let's go tonight.

WIN. Seattle.

SHAWNA. L.A.

WIN. The Grand Canyon.

SHAWNA. Okay. That's halfway there.

WIN. You don't even know me.

SHAWNA. I know a hero when I see one. Do you know how long I've been looking for a real hero? All my life, that's how long. Do you like crumb cake? I love crumb cake, especially homemade. I'll make us some. You got any ingredients?

WIN. I don't think so.

SHAWNA. You want me to stay, don't you? I'll look out for you. Hey, I can be your agent. Maybe you can have your own series. *(Sings.)* "Nightshade. Nightshade. Nightshade."

WIN. Shawna. Nightshade isn't real. She's a character on TV.

SHAWNA. I know that. But that doesn't mean she isn't real.

WIN. Shhhh… *(WIN turns up police radio. Listens. It is an announcement of a fire in progress.)* I gotta go.

SHAWNA. Where?

WIN. There's a fire downtown.

SHAWNA. So? What does that have to do with you?

WIN. I won't know until I get there. I won't be long.

SHAWNA. I'm going with you.

WIN. No, you're not.

SHAWNA. Please?

WIN. No, Shawna.

SHAWNA. You think you can stop me?

WIN. Okay, okay, but stay back from the fire.

(LIGHTS cross-fade. SOUNDS of a dog barking. TV NEWS MUSIC. PROJECTIONS.)

CASH MCKENZIE. And now a human-interest story. Winston Lawrence, hero of Woodlawn Park, has assisted in another rescue. When fire broke out downtown at Los Hermanos Grocery, firefighters arrived at the scene within minutes and the fire was quickly brought under control. No one paid much attention to the young man who stood nearby with other onlookers, holding a gray and white Shih Tzu, belonging to Raphael Jimenez, the owner of the grocery store. Mr. Jimenez, did you know that Hector had escaped from the building?

RAPHAEL JIMENEZ. No, I thought he was a goner. I was crying 'cause I love this dog, you know, and I didn't know if he got out.

CASH MCKENZIE. Tell us what happened, Mr. Jimenez.

RAPHAEL JIMENEZ. I was crying, like I say, you know, poor Hector, he's gonna burn and like that. Then I see this kid holding Hector and he's alive.

CASH MCKENZIE. You mean Win Lawrence.

RAPHAEL JIMENEZ. Sí. I didn't know who it was until later, but this Winston saw Hector shivering in the middle of the street so he rescued him and brought him back to me. It was a miracle.

CASH MCKENZIE. Why do you say that, Mr. Jimenez?

RAPHAEL JIMENEZ. You see, Hector's a Taurus, that's his sign, and tonight la luna is in Capricorn. That's a… como se dice…fortunate combination.

CASH MCKENZIE. I see.

RAPHAEL JIMENEZ. Mrs. Cash, I was so happy. I was hugging and kissing him. My sister gave him to me last year for Christmas.

CASH MCKENZIE. Do you expect Hector to make a full recovery?

RAPHAEL JIMENEZ. He is at the animal hospital for the smoke he breathed. But the doctors say he will be fine in a few days.

CASH MCKENZIE. What would you like to say to the young man who saved your dog's life?

RAPHAEL JIMENEZ. I like to say thank you, thank you. You are my hero…and Hector's, too.

CASH MCKENZIE. Thank you, Mr. Jimenez, and we wish Hector a speedy recovery. Payton?

PAYTON POWERS. Seems we have a superhero in our midst, Cash.

CASH MCKENZIE. That's the buzz, Payton.

PAYTON POWERS. And now, is your teenager a hero? How parents can instill heroic qualities in their own sons and daughters.

(LIGHTS cross-fade. PROJECTIONS out. Distant sirens. Scene of the Los Hermanos Grocery fire. SHAWNA sits nearby, out of earshot. LIEUTENANT JUDSON paces.)

JO. Now you listen to me, kid. You are not a firefighter. You don't have any training, you don't have any equipment and you don't have any right to be here. We are the firefighters, not you. You are not welcome here. Do I make myself clear? *(Pause.)* Do I make myself clear? Because next time you're gonna get more than a lecture.

WIN. I didn't do anything wrong.

JO. It's called obstructing firefighting operations and it's a class-A misdemeanor. That carries a sentence of up to one year. That's what they'll charge you with if you keep this up.

WIN. Thanks for the warning. Can I go now?

JO. Okay. I'm sorry. Sometimes I get a little carried away. Tact isn't my best quality.

WIN. You could have fooled me.

JO. What are you doing here? *(Silence.)* I saw you yesterday at that car fire, too. What's going on with you? Why are you chasing fires?

WIN. I don't know.

JO. Yes, you do. And I know you do, so you might as well tell me before they accuse you of being an arsonist.

WIN. I'm not an arsonist.
JO. That's what they're gonna think.
WIN. I'd never start a fire. I wanna help, that's all.
JO *(sighs)*. I know this hero stuff is intoxicating, kid, but you gotta stay out of the way. *(Silence.)*
WIN. I helped Hector.
JO *(laughs)*. You got grit, kid. I'll give you that. *(Pause.)* Hey, I gave you the lecture and you took it. Now take a compliment. You got grit. *(Silence.)*
WIN. I hate grits.
JO. You got courage, kid, cohones. *(Silence.)* How you getting along? Since the fire.
WIN. Fine.
JO. Oh, man. Denial ain't just a river in Egypt. You're talking to me. I was there. Fine is not an answer to my question.
WIN. Okay, I'm not fine.
JO. That's right. You having flashbacks?
WIN. I guess.
JO. Feeling scared all the time?
WIN. I'm not scared.
JO. Weird dreams?
WIN. Yeah. Okay. Really weird. I'm in the house again and the fire's everywhere.
JO. Tell me.
WIN. I'm running up the stairs and everything goes dark and I can't see. It's like someone throws a blanket over me and I get all tangled up and I can't move. I see my mom's face through the smoke and it's...it's all...I can't...
JO. Okay. Okay.
WIN. But I'll stop them. I'll make them go away.

JO. They won't go away. Not for a while.

WIN. Don't be too sure.

JO. Social Services looking out for you?

WIN. They said my brother could have temporary custody until a relative arrives.

JO. So who's coming?

WIN. I don't know.

JO. Where's your dad!

WIN. I don't have a dad. I don't know who he is or where he is. *(Silence.)*

JO. Listen, kid, I'm sorry about what happened, about your mom.

WIN. It's not your fault.

JO. I'm sorry anyway. I feel bad I had to stop you from getting her out. I know how it feels not to be able to get to somebody.

WIN. Was your mom in a fire?

JO. No, smart ass. I lost my partner. The floor dropped out from under him. There was nothing I could do. *(Silence.)*

WIN. I'm sorry.

JO *(sighs)*. Come here. *(She waits.)* Come here. You did everything you could. You know that, don't you?

WIN. I guess.

JO. No guessing about it. You damn near killed me trying to get to her. It wasn't your fault, do you hear me?

WIN. How do you know that?

JO. I'm psychic. *(Pause.)* I'm kidding. *(The two share a smile.)* Do you know what caused the fire?

WIN. It was an accident. No one started it.

JO. Whoa. I didn't say someone started it. *(Pause.)* Did you know your mom's bedroom door was locked? We had to break it down. Is that why you were so desperate to get to her? You locked her door?

WIN. No. I didn't lock the door.

JO. Somebody did. *(Silence.)* Okay, tell me this: Did the door lock from the outside or the inside?

WIN. I don't know. You could lock it from the inside or the outside. Whoever had the key.

JO. So who had the key?

WIN. I don't know.

JO. Was your mom afraid of someone or something? Was she trying to keep someone out?

WIN. I don't know. I don't know.

JO. Was your mom upset, desperate over something? Is it possible she locked the door?

WIN. Are you saying she was trying to kill herself?

JO. I don't want to upset you, kid, but it's possible. I've seen it before.

WIN. No. No way. She has some problems but she's getting better.

JO. What kind of problems?

WIN. I don't want to talk about it.

JO. Okay. Maybe the investigators will turn something up.

WIN. Investigators?

JO. There'll be an investigation, kid, so if you know something, anything, you better talk to the police. Don't be waiting for them to come to you. *(Pause.)* Are you taking this in?

WIN. Yes.

JO. Okay. Here's my number. You can call me if you want.

WIN. What for?

JO. What for? Is it such a foreign idea that you might need some help?

WIN. I can handle this.

JO. You're the oldest sixteen-year-old kid I ever met, you know that? Just call me if you need help. I'll be around.

WIN *(takes the number and puts it in his pocket)*. Thanks.

JO. Come here. Where you staying?

WIN. Parkside Hotel.

JO. The old Parkside. That's the best they could do for you?

WIN. They give us a stipend for food.

JO. Yeah, junk food. Listen, kid, my shift's over at three. You'll come have dinner at my place tonight. I'll pick you up at six sharp. Tell your brother. He could probably use some power food.

WIN. I got plans. I can't make it.

JO. Oh, you got plans? Cancel 'em. And you can bring your girlfriend over there, too.

WIN. Shawna? She's not my girlfriend.

JO. She's looking at you like she's your girlfriend. You better pay attention, kid, she'll get away from you. Six o'clock. And stay away from fires!

WIN. Hey, Jo. My mom didn't set the fire and she wasn't trying to kill herself. She was great. The best mom anybody could want. She loved me, all right? She took care of me and paid the bills and ironed my shirts. She came to all my brother's games.

JO. You don't have to explain, kid, I saw how much you love her. *(Silence.)* You remind me a lot of a crazy-ass kid I used to know.

WIN. Oh, yeah? What happened to him?

JO. He turned into me.

*(LIGHTS cross-fade. TV NEWS MUSIC. Skewed PRO-
JECTIONS. During the following, WIN takes JO's number out of his pocket and unfolds it. KURT sees it, grabs
it. WIN grabs it back, returns it to his pocket.)*

PAYTON POWERS. Winston Lawrence, the sixteen-
year-old Woodlawn Park teenager who has become a local hero, is about to receive an unusual gift. Joining me
today is Citizen's National Bank Executive Vice Presi-
dent, Celia Branch. Tell us the unusual circumstances
surrounding this gift.

MS. BRANCH. Thank you for having me on the program,
Payton. We received a call from a bank patron who read
about Mr. Lawrence in the paper and decided to make a
contribution in the amount of $10,000 to his future. He
asked only that the gift be anonymous.

PAYTON POWERS. Can you tell us why this anonymous
donor would reward Win Lawrence in particular?

MS. BRANCH. Our patron was impressed not only with
Win's dedication to his family, but by his humble atti-
tude throughout this ordeal. When our patron found out
that Mr. Lawrence is an honor student, that gave him the
idea to offer this scholarship.

PAYTON POWERS. And I understand that Citizen's National Bank has an announcement as well.

MS. BRANCH. Yes, indeed. Citizen's National Bank is de-
lighted to match our donor's contribution, making the total award for Mr. Lawrence's education $20,000. You
know, Payton, one hears so much negativity about
young people today. It's refreshing to see a young person who exemplifies our finest family values.

PAYTON POWERS. We join you in wishing Win Lawrence the brightest of futures. Indeed, he demonstrates the best in America's youth.

(LIGHTS cross-fade. PROJECTIONS out. JO JUDSON's home. After dinner. Nightshade theme plays, then fades.)

SHAWNA. So then this guy, Giorgio, kidnaps Ben. Nightshade, she goes psycho because if she hadn't told Ben where the manuscripts were, Giorgio wouldn't have kidnapped him in the first place. So she conjures up the Seer, this guy who can see the future and he says, "I will tell you where to find your beloved but you will pay a price." He wants her. They all do. Who wouldn't. But she'd do anything for Ben. So she promises the Seer she'll do whatever he asks but we won't know what it is for sure until the next episode.

WIN. Let me guess. The Seer tells Nightshade where Giorgio is holding Ben and she goes there and kicks Giorgio's butt and saves him. Totally predictable. And then they kiss. Show's over.

SHAWNA. What! You got something against kissing?

WIN. I got something against phony superheroes.

SHAWNA. Nightshade isn't phony. She's a hero. And so are you, whether you like it or not.

WIN. I don't like it.

SHAWNA. What's the matter with you? You're famous and you don't even appreciate it. Some people'd give their right arm to be famous. Even for a little while. Think of it. You can have anything. Be anything.

WIN. My house burned down and my mom's in the hospital, Shawna.

SHAWNA. I know that and no one's sorrier than I am, but why can't something good come out of it? I mean, that's okay, isn't it, Jo?

JO. I guess it's always okay to look for something good.

SHAWNA. Take a bad situation and turn it into a good one. That's what my mom says.

JO. I like your mom already and I haven't even met her.

SHAWNA. She's all about life learning and so am I. Life's all about opportunity. That's what my mom says. Think of it, Win. You could get your own TV series, anything you want.

WIN. I don't want a TV series. You do.

SHAWNA. You're right about that. That'd kick ass. I'd love to have a TV series.

JO. I've got a thing or two I'd like to say to the world.

WIN. You guys are so full of it.

SHAWNA. What?

WIN. Being famous isn't what you think. It's not about role models and doing good. It's about taking advantage of people. Making something out of nothing to make money. It's like a nightmare you can't wake up from. They make you into someone you're not, turn you into a phony and everyone believes it. *(Silence.)*

SHAWNA. So what, you're famous.

WIN. Never mind. Forget it.

SHAWNA. What'd I say? I didn't mean anything.

JO. If you feel they got the wrong idea about you, maybe you should do something about it.

WIN. Like what?

JO. I don't know, show them who you really are. Then you wouldn't be a phony.

SHAWNA. That's a great idea. Go on TV and show them the real Win Lawrence. Then they'll love you even more.

WIN. I can't do that.

JO. Why not?

WIN. I don't want to go on TV anymore, okay?

JO. It was just an idea.

WIN. I've had my fifteen minutes and I'm done.

SHAWNA. What a waste.

WIN. Everyone on TV is either a total hero or a total bad guy. That's bull. People are good *and* bad.

SHAWNA. Oh, is that right? And what did you do that's bad?

JO. I'd like to hear this.

WIN. Nothing.

SHAWNA. You never did anything bad?

WIN. I didn't say that.

SHAWNA. Then tell. Come on. I'll tell you what I did bad.

WIN. Skipped school.

SHAWNA. Of course.

WIN. What else?

SHAWNA. You go first.

WIN. No.

SHAWNA. Must be pretty bad.

WIN. Just the usual.

SHAWNA. Cut class, littered, ran a stop sign?

WIN. Of course.

SHAWNA. What else?

WIN. Forged a signature…

JO. Hey, that's impressive.

SHAWNA. Told a lie?

WIN. No.

SHAWNA. You never told a lie?

WIN. No.

SHAWNA. You mean if I wore this really ugly dress and asked how it looked on me you'd say disgusting?

WIN. No.

SHAWNA. Well, it'd be a lie then, wouldn't it?

WIN. That doesn't count.

SHAWNA. Why not?

WIN. Because it's a lie that doesn't hurt anybody.

SHAWNA. Nightshade lies to the bad guys to throw them off or get information. But that's okay.

JO. So that kind of lie is all right.

SHAWNA. Well, yeah. Sure. Depends on why you told the lie and what happens. There's good lies and bad lies.

JO. But who decides what lies are good and what lies are bad?

SHAWNA. The person who tells the lie has to decide.

JO. Then it's okay to tell a bad lie to protect someone?

WIN. This is a stupid conversation.

JO. I think it's right to the point.

SHAWNA. Sometimes you tell a good lie to help somebody and then it turns out to be a bad lie. But what matters is what you tried to do. What's in your heart.

WIN. You're wrong. There's no such thing as a good lie. They're all bad. *(Silence.)* Could we change the subject?

JO. But don't you think intent is important? Maybe more important than the outcome.

WIN. You mean the end justifies the means?

JO. No, I mean that you can't always predict how things are going to work out. But whatever happens, what's important is that you try to do what's right. Wouldn't you agree? I mean, no matter what the outcome. That's the only way you can live with yourself.

WIN. Spare me the lecture, all right?

JO. Sorry. I got carried away.

SHAWNA. What's with you, Mr. Cranky? This is fun.

WIN. I don't want to talk about it, Shawna.

SHAWNA. "I don't want to talk about it." Okay. Let's talk about adventure. In Sedona.

WIN. Shawna.

SHAWNA. We can tell her. She's a firefighter. She has adventures every day.

JO. I wouldn't exactly call it adventures.

SHAWNA. Me and Win, we want to have adventures. Show her the maps.

WIN. She doesn't want to see the maps.

JO. Sure I do, I love maps.

SHAWNA. See? *(SHAWNA gets the maps.)*

WIN. It's just an idea.

SHAWNA. He's got wanderlust. Isn't that a great word? Wanderlust.

WIN. Did you know that there's a road in California that runs along the cliffs overlooking the ocean? The Pacific Coast Highway, it's called.

SHAWNA. It goes all the way down to L.A. I want us to go there.

JO. What's this red line, here?

SHAWNA. That's his favorite route.

WIN. You start in Tucson, Arizona. You're in the desert— hot and dry, lizards and scorpions and cactus everywhere. Then you go north until you reach Sedona. That's where they have the red rock canyons, rock formations like stacked-up plates.

SHAWNA. And they're really red.

WIN. The air is cooler and rich people live there. Then you go about an hour and you're in Flagstaff, where they have pine-needle forests and mountains and skiing. It's like being in three different countries in four hours.

SHAWNA. We're gonna go there first. On a motorcycle.

WIN. It's called a bike, Shawna. But we're not going, so it doesn't matter.

JO. Why not? It's not impossible.

SHAWNA. Anything can happen. If you watched Nightshade you'd know that. It's a microcosm for the whole world. Everything's in there.

WIN. They don't have nuclear physicists.

SHAWNA. Yes, they do. They had an episode where these crazy scientists were trying to implant a nuclear device in Nightshade's brain.

WIN. Never mind.

JO. Do they have opera singers?

WIN. Yeah, they don't have opera singers.

SHAWNA. Wait, I'm thinking.

WIN. You said they have everything.

SHAWNA. They do. Give me a minute. One time there was a singer who was being stalked by a crazed groupie.

WIN. Yeah, but not an opera singer.

SHAWNA. So? She was a singer.

JO. I guess Nightshade falls short of "everything," huh, Win.

WIN. Yeah, I guess Nightshade falls short of everything.

SHAWNA. Shut up, you guys. You don't even watch.

JO. How do you know? "Into this world of crime and criminals there is one who harnesses the power of good."

SHAWNA. Oh, my God. *(JO and SHAWNA do an improvised performance of the Nightshade theme.)*

JO & SHAWNA.
    The grade is A in this charade
    This escapade of soul arcade
    Nightshade,
    Nightshade,
    Nightshade.

WIN. You two are scaring me.
JO. Come on, join in.
WIN. Not if my life depended on it.
JO. Come on.
SHAWNA. Yeah. Come on.

(During the following the two women pull WIN to his feet. JO and SHAWNA continue their performance of the Nightshade theme finally drawing WIN into the singing. At the end, SHAWNA and JO cut out leaving an embarrassed WIN singing by himself.)

JO & SHAWNA (& WIN).
    She will invade your sick parade
    She's unafraid of masquerade
    Nightshade
    Be afraid
    Nightshade
    Be afraid
    Nightshade

(LIGHTS cross-fade. TV NEWS MUSIC. PROJEC-TIONS.)

CASH MCKENZIE. ...and in a related story, Marianne Lawrence, forty-one, died tonight at Mercy Hospital from injuries sustained in the fire that ripped through her Woodlawn Park home Tuesday night. She is survived by her son, Winston Lawrence, sixteen, and his brother, Kurt Lawrence, eighteen. The investigation as to the cause of the fire is ongoing.

(LIGHTS cross-fade. PROJECTIONS out. The SOUND of WIN's MOTHER calling him as if from far away. Motel room. Police band radio blares.)

SHAWNA. Win? Are you all right? *(WIN does not answer.)* Win! I said are you all right?
WIN *(turns radio lower)*. Shawna, go home.
SHAWNA. I am home.
WIN. This isn't anyone's home.
SHAWNA. My home is wherever you are.
WIN. If you really knew me you'd be out of here so fast...
SHAWNA. Oh, yeah?
WIN. Yeah.
SHAWNA. Try me.
WIN. I can't.
SHAWNA. Why not? You think if you tell me I'll disappear?
WIN. Probably.
SHAWNA. All right. Don't tell me.
WIN. Just like that?
SHAWNA. I don't want to know. Besides, I trust you.

WIN. You shouldn't.

SHAWNA. Well, I do. If you don't want to tell me you don't have to. That's what Nightshade would say. She'd never box someone she loved in a corner.

WIN. I don't want to hear about Nightshade. *(Silence.)*

SHAWNA. Did I tell you I met your mom once?

WIN. No, you never told me.

SHAWNA. I didn't have the chance.

WIN. Where?

SHAWNA. Downtown at the pharmacy. I stole this lipstick. You know, slipped it in my pocket. I got caught. The manager saw me. Some thief, huh? So I made up this huge lie about forgetting it was in my pocket and how I didn't really mean to steal it. He totally didn't believe me. He was gonna call my parents. But then your mom, she was just there, like this fairy godmother or guardian angel or something. She said she knew me. That I was from a nice family and wouldn't make up a story like that. And the manager let me go. I couldn't believe it.

WIN. She was always doing stuff like that.

SHAWNA. Then it turned out she really did know my family. She and my mom went to high school together. They used to be friends.

WIN. But not anymore.

SHAWNA. I asked my mom about her but she just said it was a long time ago and things change. *(Silence.)* I never stole anything again after that. Never. *(Silence.)*

WIN. Shawna, what if I told you that it's all a lie? I'm really not a hero.

SHAWNA. You mean the fire and all that?

WIN. What if I didn't save anybody?

SHAWNA. But you did. You saved me.

WIN. That's not what I mean.

SHAWNA. "Leave her alone," you said to those losers, "What's she ever done to you?" You have no idea how much I needed someone to care about me just a little and you did. Do you think anything else matters after that?

WIN. Shawna…

SHAWNA. Shut up, okay? You don't have to say anything. I know it's all just a fantasy. I'm not stupid.

WIN. It's all lies.

SHAWNA. So what? I don't care about that. I care about you. *(Pause.)* Just let me have this, okay? *(WIN lies down. SHAWNA turns off the radio, covers WIN.)* I'm never gonna be like Nightshade, I know that. I'm not famous, I'm not buff. I'm not even pretty. But you… you're special. Everyone thinks so. *(She lies down beside him, holds him.)* Tell me you'll be all right. You have to be all right. Because if you aren't then the whole world sucks.

WIN. Shawna?

SHAWNA. Yeah?

WIN. Want to run away?

SHAWNA. Yeah. Let's go tonight. Niagara Falls.

WIN. New York.

SHAWNA. Disneyland.

WIN. The Grand Canyon.

SHAWNA. Okay. *(Silence.)* Win?

WIN. Yeah.

SHAWNA. You know I can't really run away with you, don't you.

WIN. Yeah, I know.

SHAWNA. But I wish I could. *(WIN turns and holds her.)*

(Outside the motel room. LIGHTS cross-fade. TV NEWS MUSIC. PROJECTIONS increase in distortion. CASH MCKENZIE and PAYTON POWERS flank WIN.)

PAYTON POWERS. Fire investigators have released a report today on the Woodlawn Park fire last Tuesday night that left Marianne Lawrence, forty-one, dead.

CASH MCKENZIE. The report confirms that the fire originated in the bedroom of the deceased, Marianne Lawrence, and states that electrical problems were not the cause of the fire, that human error was involved.

WIN. It wasn't an error. It was an accident.

PAYTON POWERS. The report falls short of naming individuals who may have been criminally responsible, but there is considerable speculation about who caused the devastating blaze.

WIN. What? No one was criminally responsible.

PAYTON POWERS. The report also contains a shocking revelation. Marianne Lawrence's bedroom door was locked when the fire broke out.

WIN. We didn't know. We didn't know there'd be a fire.

CASH MCKENZIE. These questions remain: Why was the bedroom door locked and who locked it?

WIN. Shut up! It's none of your business. This is my family, not yours!

CASH MCKENZIE. At the center of the allegations is Marianne Lawrence. According to the autopsy report, Lawrence's blood alcohol level was point one nine when she was brought into the emergency room...

WIN. It wasn't her fault. It wasn't.

PAYTON POWERS. ...leading to speculation that her alcoholism contributed to the cause of the fire.

WIN. That's a lie. You're lying about my mother. She wasn't an alcoholic. She wasn't!

PAYTON POWERS. Brothers Kurt and Winston Lawrence have not yet been named as suspects but may be interviewed by police. Is Winston Lawrence, the so-called hero of Woodlawn Park, a young man protecting the memory of his mother, or is he withholding crucial information from authorities?

CASH MCKENZIE. That remains to be seen. But one thing about heroes—they tell the truth. Back to you, Payton...

(LIGHTS cross-fade. PROJECTIONS out. The motel room. SOUND of police band radio. The phone rings. Rings again. Again.)

KURT. Don't answer it.

WIN. Do you think I'm stupid? I'm not talking to those people ever again. Are they still out there?

KURT. About a dozen of 'em. Like vultures. *(WIN turns up police band radio.)* Will you turn that thing off?

WIN. No.

KURT. Turn it off. It's driving me crazy.

WIN. I can't help that.

KURT. Well, I don't think I can help kicking your ass.

WIN. Go ahead.

KURT. I oughta. What are you doing anyway?

WIN. Putting in these batteries.

KURT. I think one flashlight's enough.

WIN. We need one for the bathroom and I want one near the bed and the door.

KURT. I thought you were supposed to be the big hero. I wonder what all those media hounds would say if they knew you're afraid of the dark?

WIN. I'm not afraid of the dark. I want to be ready, just in case.

KURT. Get over yourself, Boy Scout. Your fifteen minutes of fame is over. And you blew it.

WIN. I didn't tell them anything.

KURT. You bawled your head off like a baby.

WIN. I did not.

KURT. Now they think you've got something to hide. And they're going to come after you. They're going to dig and dig and dig until they break you. I told you, you've gotta toughen up. You can't let them think you're weak. You gotta be a man and keep your mouth shut. We don't owe anybody anything.

WIN. What about Mom?

KURT. Forget her. All our lives it's been you and me. Nobody cared about us before. Why should anybody care now? I just hope they don't take back the money.

WIN. I don't want the money.

KURT. Oh. The Boy Scout has a guilty conscience. Okay. Give back the money. And while you're at it, tell 'em all about how Mom was a drunk and a slut…

WIN. Shut up, Kurt.

KURT. …and we had to watch her every minute so she wouldn't kill somebody with her car or drive herself off a cliff. That oughta make a good story. The TV people will love that.

WIN. Shut up!

KURT. Or you could tell 'em how she used to get ugly and bash me around for fun until I got too big. Tell 'em how I'd stand between the two of you so she wouldn't hurt you when she was psycho. Tell 'em how we never knew what she'd do so we were ashamed to be seen with her. That'd make colorful TV viewing. *(WIN charges at KURT. The two struggle. KURT gains control.)* You don't get it, do you? The fire was the best thing that ever happened to us. We're free, Win. For the first time in our lives we're free from her. I can go to college and not have to be worried every minute that she got ugly with you. You can make some friends and have a life. You don't have to do mom detail ever again. What did she ever do for us? Huh? Nothing.

WIN. That's not true.

KURT. She was nothing but trouble.

WIN. You're glad she's dead.

KURT. I guess I am. Now I've only got you and me to worry about.

WIN. Tell you what. Now you've got two less people to worry about.

KURT. Come on, Win. I didn't mean it like that. It was an accident.

WIN. Then stop celebrating.

KURT. I just want us to have a life.

WIN. I want her not to have died. I want her back.

KURT. You don't want her back. You want that picture you painted of her to be real. You want what you pretended she was. You never saw the truth, Boy Scout. It was ugly.

WIN. She didn't mean it, Kurt.

KURT. Yeah. Forgive her, like always. Even for this.

WIN. She's dead.

KURT. It was her own fault.

WIN. It wasn't her fault that we locked the door. We killed her, Kurt.

KURT. Shut up. Don't talk like that. It was an accident. End of story.

WIN. Can't you feel sorry at all?

KURT. Nope. *(Silence.)* Think about what we have to lose. If the truth comes out, it all comes out. All of it. Don't get any ideas about telling the truth because of stupid Boy Scout guilt. Just leave it alone. You got it, Win? I'm not going backwards and neither are you. You owe me this. And you know it.

(WIN turns up the volume on the police band radio as LIGHTS cross-fade. TV NEWS MUSIC.)

PAYTON POWERS. This portion of the news is brought to you by Bracknell, Shapiro, Weber and Hook. Accidental injuries deserve compensation for pain and suffering. Bracknell, Shapiro, Weber and Hook. Putting your life back in order.

CASH MCKENZIE. In the local news, Winston Lawrence, the hero of Woodlawn Park, is being sought for questioning about the death of his mother, Marianne Lawrence, and the fire that destroyed their home. The fire marshall's report has raised questions as to the cause of that fire and the strange mystery surrounding the locked bedroom door that contributed to the death of Marianne Lawrence. Although he has not been charged with any crime, questions remain: Is the hero of Woodlawn Park really heroic? Or has he used this tragic situation to his own advantage? And we'll be back after this brief message.

(LIGHTS cross-fade. PROJECTIONS out. The SOUND of WIN's MOTHER calling his name. JO JUDSON's home. WIN carries the duffle bag.)

JO. You going someplace?
WIN. I came to say goodbye.
JO. Where you going?
WIN. I don't know. Anywhere.
JO. Just disappear. Is that the plan?
WIN. Pretty much. The insurance money came in.
JO. I didn't even know what insurance was at your age.
WIN. Skip the lecture, all right.
JO. I heard the police want to talk to you.
WIN. Kurt says we should keep our mouths shut.
JO. What do you say?
WIN. It's none of their business.
JO. Have you talked to a lawyer?
WIN. We don't need a lawyer. We haven't done anything.
JO. Okay, okay. You don't have to be so defensive.
WIN. I'm not defensive.
JO. Is Kurt going with you?
WIN. No.
JO. Ah. You've had a difference of opinion.
WIN. You could say that.
JO. So you're just leaving him behind. That's pretty serious, kid. He's all you got left. *(Silence.)* We got us a giant mess now, don't we. Come here. *(Pause.)* Come here. I'm sorry about your mom.
WIN. It's okay.

JO. It's not okay. Listen to me. Terrible things have happened to you. There's no getting around it. You just have to go through it. *(Silence.)*

WIN. I don't want to go through it. Not anymore.

JO. Did you set the fire, kid?

WIN. No.

JO. Did Kurt? *(Silence.)*

WIN. I don't know.

JO. So that's what you're running away from.

WIN. You don't know anything about anything. You're not my mother, all right? My mother's dead. She's dead. I don't have to answer to you.

JO. You're right. I'm not your mother. But I care about you. God knows why, 'cause you are one miserable kid if ever I saw one. Something's eating you up inside. Why don't you let me help you?

WIN. Why would you do that?

JO. Because people pass by each other everyday. They don't look. They don't see the pain. They don't know what's goin' on with those people and they don't care. Just as long as they're safe. Just as long as their world is in tact. Somebody gets in an accident, there's danger, everyone just stands there, staring at it like it's on TV. And that's a tragedy. You ever seen a man on fire with a crowd standing around watching?

WIN. I got no idea what you're talking about.

JO. You didn't pass by, kid. You didn't just stand there. *(Pause.)*

WIN. That's crap and you know it.

JO. Give me a break. It's the only argument I got left.

WIN. I'm gonna remember that. I know it's crap but it's all I got left.

JO. You like it, it's yours. *(Silence.)*

WIN. I gotta go.

JO. If you run, this thing'll follow you and you might never get yourself out from under it. How about you stay and we'll figure something out.

WIN. Like what?

JO. I don't know. I'm thinking on it.

WIN. Take care of yourself, okay?

JO *(holds out a key)*. Here.

WIN. A key?

JO. To the front door. I figure if you ever need it, you'll have it handy.

WIN. I could stay here?

JO. You do your own laundry. *(Silence.)*

WIN. You'd do that for me?

JO. I think I just did.

WIN. No. I can't take it.

JO. Why not? I got a big place. *(Silence.)* Gets to you, doesn't it. When somebody cares.

WIN. I'm not who you think I am.

JO. I have a pretty good idea who you are. You're the one who's not so sure. *(Silence. WIN turns away. JO tries to comfort WIN. He shrugs her off.)* What is it with you guys? It's like you've got this unwritten law, thou shalt not talk. Why do you always have to keep everything locked up? I just don't get it.

WIN. That's right. You wouldn't understand.

JO. Because I'm not a guy?

WIN. For one thing.

JO. Give me a break. I know all about guys. I live in the world of guys. I eat, sleep and fight fires with guys. Hell, most days I feel like I am a guy. Stay tough. Don't show your feelings. They'll think you're weak. Hell, you're not even allowed to have feelings, because if you crack open that door there'll be such a flood you might drown in it—all those ugly emotions you've been keeping locked up. But you feel 'em, don't you, even if you deny it. Love, anger, fear, guilt. I know your mom hurt you, but everyone's not like her, Win. Why don't you take a chance. Trust someone else.

WIN. Because if I know one thing for sure, it's you can't trust anybody. They'll let you down every single time. You think you got 'em figured out and then they turn on you.

JO. Like your mom?

WIN. Leave her out of this.

JO. You said it yourself. I'm not your mother. I'm just a grown-up crazy-ass kid who cares about you.

WIN. Leave me alone.

JO. You say that but you don't mean it. I know you're scared.

WIN. I'm not scared.

JO. Yes, you are.

WIN. I said I'm not scared.

JO. Well, I am. I'm scared enough for both of us. Big, decorated, pumped-up firefighter. I'm scared all the time. That siren goes off I get this knot in my stomach feels like I'm gonna burst wide open. When I'm riding in the rig, when I look up and see the site and know I'm going in there when everyone else is running out. When my partner and I are working in burning buildings—buildings that are fully involved—heat so intense you feel your skin sizzling underneath your gear. I'm scared I'll get separated or disoriented so I can't find my way out or the floor'll collapse again and we'll be trapped. *(Pause.)* You know what I'm most afraid of? That one time fear'll get the best of me and I'll turn tail and run somewhere where there aren't any fires. Somewhere I'm safe from all of it. Let me tell you, kid, everybody's scared. They just don't want to admit it. Fear is nothing to be ashamed of. It's crazy not to be afraid in this world. *(Silence.)*

WIN. Everyone thinks I'm this big hero. I don't wanna be around when they find out the truth.

JO. Nobody's perfect. Even heroes.

WIN. I'm the opposite of a hero.

JO. Well, that depends on your definition. See, there's two kinds of heroes—the kind who put their lives in danger to help somebody, the kind you read about in the papers and see on the news. Then there's the everyday heroes. They do the quiet acts of bravery nobody ever hears about. Like doing the right thing, not just when it's easy, but when it's inconvenient, when it's scary. I think that's pretty heroic, don't you? *(Silence. WIN starts to leave.)* What you do now will tell us what you're made of. Whether this hero label fits or not.

WIN. You never let up, do you?

JO. Nope.

WIN. Can I keep the key?

JO. You bet.

WIN. Thanks.

JO. I'm here if you need me. *(Silence.)*

WIN. Don't try to stop me.

JO. I won't.

WIN. Don't try to make me feel guilty.

JO. I won't.

WIN. Don't try to find me.

JO. I won't.

WIN. You won't?

JO. I won't. *(Silence.)*

WIN. She was right.

JO. Who?

WIN. My mom. She used to say she missed her chance. Keep your bags packed, she'd say, and when you see your chance come sliding down the highway, grab hold of it and run or it'll slip away from you. All my life I've been waiting for my chance and now it's gonna slip away.

JO. Maybe not.

WIN. I'm watching it disappear.

JO. There'll be other chances. *(Silence.)*

WIN. I loved my mom. I was supposed to take care of her. Look out for her. She was so helpless. I couldn't save her from herself and I couldn't save her from the fire. I tried. I'm sorry. I'm sorry I didn't save her. I'm sorry.

JO. It wasn't your fault.

WIN. That's the biggest lie of all. *(Silence.)* We locked the door, Jo. Me and Kurt locked her in.

(LIGHTS cross-fade. TV NEWS MUSIC. PROJECTIONS increase in distortion.)

PAYTON POWERS. With us today is Dr. Florence Krakauer, professor of Clinical Psychology at Yale University and author of the book *Heroes Defined.* Welcome, Dr. Krakauer. There's been a great deal of talk recently about heroes, who and what they are. How do we identify a real hero?

DR. KRAKAUER. Simply defined, a hero is someone who puts others before him or herself, often at great risk.

(WIN enters, carrying duffel bag.)

KURT. Where've you been?

WIN. I've been at Jo's.

KURT. What's up with you two? I thought Shawna was your girlfriend.

WIN. Why do you do that?

KURT. What?

WIN. Make everything dirty.

KURT. Everything is dirty.

WIN. Maybe to you. It's not like that between me and Jo.

KURT. What do you want?

WIN. I want to know what's up with you. I don't even know you anymore.

KURT. Maybe you never knew me in the first place.

PAYTON POWERS. Would you agree, Dr. Krakauer, that a hero is someone who is willing to face danger for a noble cause?

DR. KRAKAUER. That's an accepted definition.

PAYTON POWERS. What makes a hero? Where does heroism come from?

DR. KRAKAUER. It's complicated. I think of it as the "impulse to the good."

WIN. I'm gonna talk to the police and I want you to go with me.

KURT. I already told you. We're not talking to the police. We'll get a lawyer.

WIN. We don't need a lawyer. We didn't break any laws.

KURT. Jo tell you that?

WIN. Yeah. So we don't have to worry about being charged with anything.

KURT. Right. Like they'll believe us. *(Silence.)* Did you tell her we locked the door?

WIN. Yes.

KURT. You idiot. I told you not to tell anybody.

WIN. She understands. I'm glad I told her.

KURT. Because you feel better now that you've got it off your chest?

WIN. Maybe. She says I can stay with her.

KURT. No way. I want you where I can keep my eye on you.

WIN. What about what I want?

KURT. You don't know what you want.

WIN. Maybe I do know. Maybe I know for the first time. I want to make my own mistakes. I don't want to go back to how it was before…worrying all the time about what people think. Scared that somebody'll find out. It's over, Kurt. I want it to be over.

PAYTON POWERS. I'm curious to know your thoughts on the hero of Woodlawn Park, in light of the shocking revelations about his home situation, his lies, and the locked bedroom door.

DR. KRAKAUER. I'm not interested in speculation, Payton. I'll leave that to the media.

PAYTON POWERS. But how do you respond to the allegations that he may have been involved in his mother's death?

DR. KRAKAUER. Like I said, I'm not interested in speculating. But whatever else Win Lawrence may or may not have done, he put his life in danger to save his brother and his mother.

PAYTON POWERS. So in spite of the investigation, would you still call Win Lawrence the hero of Woodland Park?

DR. KRAKAUER. I don't care for labels, Payton. It's inappropriate for us to conjecture about what might have happened. How can we ever know...

PAYTON POWERS. I'm sorry, Dr. Krakauer. We're out of time.

WIN. Will you go with me?

KURT. Leave me out of this. You were the one that wanted to go out. That's why we locked the door.

WIN. What? It was your idea.

KURT. To help you out.

WIN. It wasn't just about what I wanted. You wanted to sleep.

KURT. Are you saying it was my fault?

WIN. Are you saying it was mine?

KURT. If the shoe fits...

WIN. Sometimes I hate you. You know that?

KURT. You wanted to meet Shawna or whatever her name is.

WIN. I didn't do it alone, Kurt. It was both of us.

KURT. What do you know about anything, Boy Scout?

WIN. Don't call me Boy Scout. Don't ever call me that again.

KURT. That's what you are. That's what you've always been. The good boy.

WIN. What does that mean?

KURT. It means that I'm sick of you thinking you're better than me.

WIN. I don't think that.

KURT. Yes, you do. And so did Mom. Anything that went wrong was my fault. It couldn't be Win. Not her perfect boy. No way. And who do you think they're gonna blame for the fire? Not the Boy Scout, that's for sure. They're gonna blame me.

WIN. It won't matter if you didn't do it.

KURT. Oh, that's nice. That's great. Even you think I killed her.

WIN. You were the one who wanted to lock the door! You wanted her out of the way. You probably even wanted her dead.

KURT. Why you little… *(KURT grabs WIN and gets in his face. His arm is raised, about to hit his brother.)* Go ahead. Hit me. Go ahead. Do it! You never cared about her! You never loved her! Not ever! *(Silence. KURT releases WIN. Folds in on himself.)* I loved her. I loved her when you were nothing but a snot-nosed kid. I remember how she used to be. I remember her and Dad. How they were together. I remember how she used to sing us to sleep at night. I remember when she was pretty. When she was the whole world. *(Silence.)* Maybe I wanted her dead, maybe I even wished she was dead, but don't say I never loved her. She was the one who didn't know anything about love. She didn't love us. Not enough to stay sober. Not even enough to stay alive. *(Silence.)* Believe me or not, I don't care.

WIN. I believe you.

KURT. I'm telling the truth.

WIN. I believe you. You're my brother.

KURT. You can count on that.

(LIGHTS cross-fade. KURT exits. TV MUSIC. PROJEC-TIONS no longer distorted.)

CASH MCKENZIE. In the local news tonight…Win Lawrence and his brother Kurt Lawrence will not be charged in the Woodlawn Park fire that decimated their home last Tuesday night. The fire has been officially ruled accidental. When Everyday attempted to reach the hero of Woodlawn Park, he was unavailable for comment. Unconfirmed sources say he was last seen with his brother, Kurt, at Junior's Harley Davidson on Highway Six, where they purchased two cross-country motorcycles. It appears that Win Lawrence and his brother have disappeared, leaving no clues as to their whereabouts and no forwarding address. No one seems to know what has happened to the hero of Woodlawn Park. Payton?

PAYTON POWERS. Coming up next: The high cost of travel: how to go the distance on a shoestring budget. Stay with us.

(LIGHTS cross-fade. PROJECTIONS out. SHAWNA hands WIN the duffle bag. They embrace. SHAWNA fades. WIN in spotlight.)

WIN. I figured something out. In between being invisible and being famous is one person. Someone who really knows you. I got that now. Jo helped me and Kurt make our get-away and resettle here. She's more of a mom to me than my real mom ever was. I still dream, but not about traveling. Not anymore. At night I dream fire dreams. I feel the red heat and smell the black smoke. I hear my mother call to me, from far away. I run toward the sound of her voice, but it keeps changing so that when I see her, when I reach out to her, she's not there and her voice starts calling me from somewhere else. Then I wake up. I lie there and wish that things had been different. That somehow I could have…fixed her, you know? Fixed everything. But now I understand that she was beyond me, like in the dreams, beyond my reach. During the day I plan. That's a different kind of dreaming. After school I climb up on the red rocks and think about how I want to be in the world. What I'll do and how I'll do it. I want to choose my life. Recognize those chances when they come sliding down the highway and grab 'em. Grab on and hold 'em tight before they slip away.

LIGHTS FADE TO BLACKOUT
END PLAY

Everyday Heroes After-play Interactive Forum

Designed and written by Laurie Brooks

At the end of the play the curtain call is held until the end of the forum. After the blackout, the facilitator, who introduces him/herself and invites the audience to participate in the Forum, greets the audience.

Agree and Disagree Statements

Facilitator: Hello. My name is _______________ and I'd like to ask you for your help. I'd like us to spend some time talking about the story we've just seen. I know I have some thoughts and questions about the people and their choices in the story. Let's begin with some opinions. I'd like to read you a series of statements. As I read each statement, stand up if you agree to show your support, or if you disagree, remain seated in protest.

1. It was not Win and Kurt's responsibility to take care of their mother.

2. It is okay to lie to protect a family member.

3. Win is right when he says, "A lie doesn't count if it doesn't hurt anybody."

4. Kurt Lawrence is a good brother to Win.

5. When something is on the news we automatically assume it is true.

6. Jo is right when she says, "Men have this unwritten rule, thou shalt not talk."

7. Win Lawrence was not really a hero.

8. The truth is more important than loyalty.

9. Anyone can be a hero.

10. Anyone can be an everyday hero.

Exploration: Lies, deceptions, half-truths and denial

Facilitator: There are over fifty lies told in *Everyday Heroes*—deceptions, half-truths and denial, when someone can't admit the truth to themselves or others, maybe because it's too painful. What are some of the lies you remember from the play?

Audience responds.

The Facilitator offers positive, neutral responses to audience members after they speak, such as, "Thank you." or "I didn't think of that."

Facilitator: Who was in denial in the play? What were they in denial about?

Audience responds.

Facilitator: Do you think that in this play one lie led to another? Which lie do you think caused the most damage?

Audience responds.

Facilitator: I'd like to give Kurt and Win a chance to speak about this. Let's ask the boys to join us.

Kurt and Win enter. They wear different clothes so it is clear they have begun their new life and we are looking back on the past.

Facilitator: How are you doing?

Boys each respond with one or two sentences about their new life. Keep it brief, specific and use clues from the play.

Facilitator: Kurt, we've been talking about your experiences during the time of the fire, and I'm wondering if you'd be willing to share some thoughts with us. Looking back on what happened, if you could take back one lie, which one would it be?

Kurt responds. His answers are brief and specific.

Facilitator: How about you, Win? Which lie would you take back?

Win responds with different thoughts.

Reflection: Unexpected Mentors

Facilitator: Sometimes random people take an interest in someone else and that changes their life. Like Jo did with Kurt and Win. I wonder how many of you here tonight have known someone whose caring changed your life, maybe someone outside the family who didn't have to care? Raise your hand if you've had that experience. That's a lot. Kurt and Win, will you share with us how Jo changed your lives?

Kurt and Win each respond with different specifics. Avoid clichés.

Facilitator: (To the audience.) I'd like to hear from you about the person who has made a difference in your life. I wish we had time to hear all your stories, but just give us a sentence or a phrase about your mentor and what that person did for you. You don't have to raise your hands, just stand if you'd like to share and take turns. Start your sentence with, "I learned or I realized…"

Facilitator steps back, allowing the audience to respond on their own.

Facilitator: Thank you for coming and thank you for sharing…

Win interrupts.

Win: Can I say something?

Facilitator: Sure. Go ahead.

Win: My mom told me to watch for my chance when it comes sliding down the highway. I'm just hoping that if you get a chance to help someone out—maybe be a mentor to someone—you'll grab onto that chance and take it before it slips away.

Kurt joins his brother to show his support.

Facilitator: Thank you, boys. And thank you for coming and thanks for being an everyday hero. Now give yourselves and the entire cast of *Everyday Heroes* a big hand.

Actors take their curtain call.

End Forum.

DIRECTOR'S NOTES

DIRECTOR'S NOTES